# WITHDRAWN
From Toronto Public Library

Big
Science Ideas

# Warm-blooded or Cold-blooded?

## Bobbie Kalman

Crabtree Publishing Company

www.crabtreebooks.com

**Big Science Ideas**

# Created by Bobbie Kalman

For Brigitte Pidduck, my university roommate, with love and gratitude
You were my role model, sister, and friend.
I'm so happy to have you back in my life again!

**Author and Editor-in-Chief**
Bobbie Kalman

**Editor**
Kathy Middleton

**Proofreader**
Crystal Sikkens

**Design**
Bobbie Kalman
Katherine Kantor
Samantha Crabtree (cover)

**Production coordinator**
Katherine Kantor

**Prepress technician**
Margaret Amy Salter

**Illustrations**
Barbara Bedell: pages 6, 18, 19
Bonna Rouse: page 30

**Photographs**
© Dreamstime.com: pages 17 (walrus),
    19 (top), 22 (bottom), 23 (except top left)
© Shutterstock.com: front and back cover,
    title page, pages 3, 4, 5, 6, 7, 8, 9, 10, 11 (right),
    12, 14, 15, 16, 17 (except walrus), 18, 19 (bottom),
    20, 21, 22 (top), 23 (top left), 24, 25, 26 (top), 27,
    28 (bottom), 30, 31
Other images by Corel and Digital Vision

**Library and Archives Canada Cataloguing in Publication**

Kalman, Bobbie, 1947-
    Warm-blooded or cold-blooded? / Bobbie Kalman.

(Big science ideas)
Includes index.
ISBN 978-0-7787-3281-5 (bound).--ISBN 978-0-7787-3301-0 (pbk.)

    1. Body temperature--Juvenile literature. 2. Body
temperature--Regulation--Juvenile literature. I. Title.
II. Series: Kalman, Bobbie, 1947- . Big science ideas.

QP135.K34 2008          j571.7'61          C2008-905727-9

**Library of Congress Cataloging-in-Publication Data**

Kalman, Bobbie.
    Warm-blooded or cold-blooded? / Bobbie Kalman.
      p. cm. -- (Big science ideas)
    Includes index.
    ISBN-13: 978-0-7787-3301-0 (pbk. : alk. paper)
    ISBN-10: 0-7787-3301-7 (pbk. : alk. paper)
    ISBN-13: 978-0-7787-3281-5 (reinforced library binding : alk. paper)
    ISBN-10: 0-7787-3281-9 (reinforced library binding : alk. paper)
    1. Body temperature--Regulation--Juvenile literature. 2. Animals--
Juvenile literature. I. Title.
    QP135.K35 2009
    612'.01426--dc22

                                                2008037689

## Crabtree Publishing Company
www.crabtreebooks.com          1-800-387-7650

**Published in Canada**
**Crabtree Publishing**
616 Welland Ave.
St. Catharines, Ontario
L2M 5V6

**Published in the United States**
**Crabtree Publishing**
PMB16A
350 Fifth Ave., Suite 3308
New York, NY  10118

**Published in the United Kingdom**
**Crabtree Publishing**
White Cross Mills
High Town, Lancaster
LA1 4XS

**Published in Australia**
**Crabtree Publishing**
386 Mt. Alexander Rd.
Ascot Vale (Melbourne)
VIC 3032

# Contents

# Warm- or cold-blooded?

People and animals are **living things** that need to keep their bodies warm. Some living things can control their **body temperatures** better than others can. Body temperature is how warm it is inside the body of a living thing.

## Warm-blooded

**Warm-blooded** animals can make heat inside their bodies. They can also cool down their bodies when their bodies are too warm. Warm-blooded animals can keep their body temperatures **constant**, or about the same most of the time.

4

# Which is which?

**Cold-blooded** animals can also warm their bodies or cool them down, but they do not do it from the inside. Their bodies are hot when the animals are in hot places and cold when they are in cold places. Which three animals on this page are warm-blooded? Which five animals are cold-blooded? Are people warm-blooded or cold-blooded? Turn the page if you do not know!

*butterfly*

*snail*

*rabbits*

*birds*

*snake*

*turtle*

**Answers:**

**Warm-blooded:** birds, rabbits, orca

**Cold-blooded:** butterfly, snake, turtle, alligator, snail

*orca*

*alligator*

5

# Warm-blooded animals

Birds and **mammals** are warm-blooded. Mammals are animals that have some hair or fur on their bodies. People are mammals, too. They are warm-blooded. Birds and mammals keep their body temperatures constant. The body temperature of a person, for example, may change a little during the day, but it is usually around 98.6°F or 37°C.

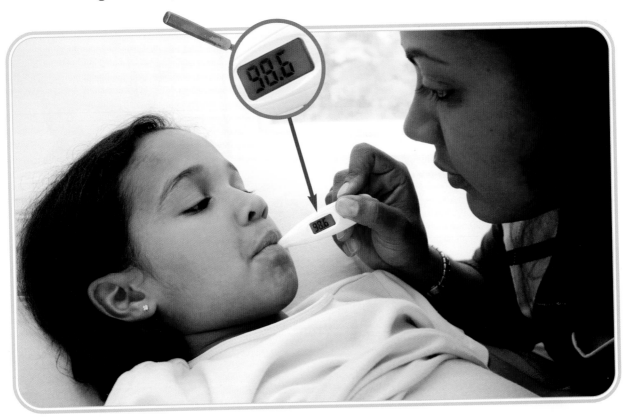

*People can check their temperatures with a thermometer. This child's temperature is 98.6°F. Is the temperature normal, or is it too high? What does a high temperature usually mean?*

6

# Different bodies

All the animals shown on this page are warm-blooded. Warm-blooded animals have different bodies, but they can all keep their bodies at a constant temperature.

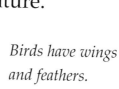

*Birds have wings and feathers.*

*Kittens are mammals that are covered in fur.*

*Elephants are huge mammals. They have hair on their bodies.*

*Dolphins are mammals that live in oceans. Their bodies are smooth for swimming.*

# Cold-blooded animals

Cold-blooded animals do not heat their bodies from the inside. Their body heat comes from the outside, and their body temperatures are not constant. They change as the temperatures of their **surroundings** change. Frogs, **reptiles**, fish, insects, and spiders, are cold-blooded animals. Most ocean animals are also cold-blooded.

*The body of the frog sitting in the sun is warm. The body of the frog in the water is much cooler.*

# Not all the same!

Cold-blooded animals have different bodies. They do not all warm or cool their bodies in the same ways. All the animals on this page are cold-blooded. Most of the animals on Earth are cold-blooded.

*Butterflies are insects. All insects are cold-blooded.*

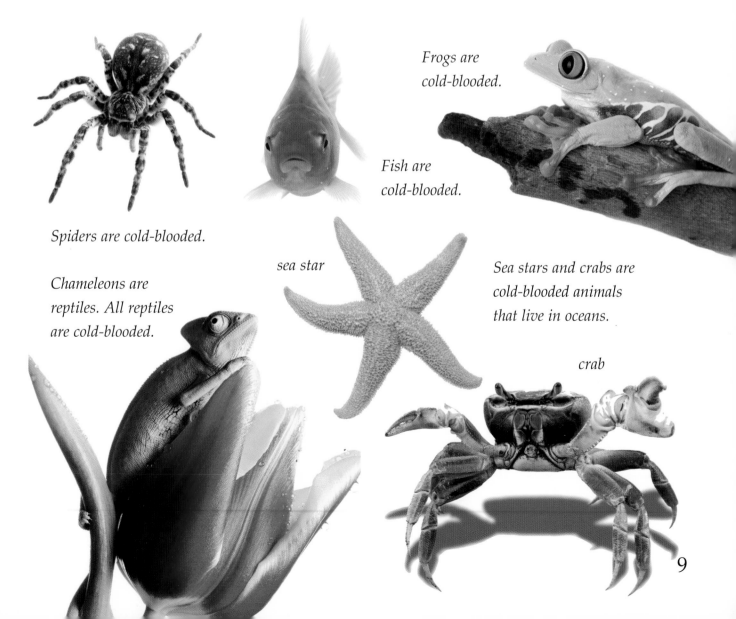

*Frogs are cold-blooded.*

*Fish are cold-blooded.*

*Spiders are cold-blooded.*

*Chameleons are reptiles. All reptiles are cold-blooded.*

sea star

*Sea stars and crabs are cold-blooded animals that live in oceans.*

crab

# Eating to keep warm

Warm-blooded animals make heat inside their bodies. To make body heat, they need to eat a lot of food. Food gives them **energy**. Energy is the power that people and animals need to breathe, grow, move, and keep warm. Most of the food that warm-blooded animals eat is used to keep their bodies warm.

# "I'm shivering!"

Warm-blooded animals are able to warm their bodies by **shivering** when they are cold. When you shiver, your body shakes to warm you up. People and animals also **huddle** together to keep one another warm. What other ways do you use to warm your body?

*This child is shivering to warm up.*

*Drinking something hot warms you up.*

*Baby penguins huddle to keep their bodies warm.*

*These monkeys are having a bath in a hot pool to warm up on a cold winter day.*

11

# Getting some sun

Warm-blooded animals need a lot of food to keep their bodies warm. Cold-blooded animals do not need as much food. They warm their bodies in different ways. Some cold-blooded animals **bask**, or take in heat, from the sun. Warm animals are active. When animals are cold, they are **sluggish**, or move slowly.

*These turtles have come out of the water to warm their bodies in the sun.*

To warm themselves in the sun, cold-blooded animals lie flat so the sun's rays will cover their bodies like a blanket. This Komodo dragon is sunbathing on a rock. Rocks get hot in the sun and stay hot. The dragon's body is being warmed both by the rock and by the sun.

Snakes also warm themselves in the sun. This snake is resting near its **den**, or home.

This iguana has made parts of its skin darker. Dark colors **absorb**, or take in, more sunlight.

# ...ping warm

...blooded animals shiver to keep warm. Some cold-blooded animals also shiver. Hummingbird moths and honeybees shiver by flapping their wings quickly. Honeybees also keep warm by crowding together.

*This hummingbird moth is flapping its wings very quickly to make heat and energy in its body.*

# Holding in heat

Some very large cold-blooded animals, such as sea turtles, can take in the sun's heat and keep it in their bodies. They can then swim in cold water and still stay warm for a long time.

*This sea turtle is sunning itself at the edge of the ocean. Its body is taking in heat.*

*After absorbing a lot of sunlight, this sea turtle is able to keep heat in its body while it is under water. When the turtle feels cold again, it can float on the surface of the ocean to get more sun.*

# Warm coats for the cold

What kind of clothes do you wear in winter? Do you wear a warm coat with a hood? Just as you need to keep warm, warm-blooded animals that live in cold places also need to keep warm. Animals do not wear clothes, so how do they keep warm?

## Freezing cold!

Not many kinds of animals can live in freezing-cold places. Animals that do live in these places have warm fur coats, thick feathers, or **blubber** to keep the heat inside their bodies and to keep out the cold. Blubber is a heavy layer of fat.

*This girl is dressed warmly, but she is still shivering from the cold. Shivering helps warm her body.*

16

Polar bears live in the Arctic, where it is very cold in winter. They have fur and a thick layer of blubber.

In winter, Arctic wolves grow white fur coats that are very warm.

Penguins live in icy Antarctica. These birds have both feathers and blubber to keep them warm.

Red foxes grow thick fur coats and bushy tails for the winter.

Walruses have tough skin and a layer of blubber. Walruses live in icy oceans, but they do not feel the cold.

17

# Changing ears

The bodies of some warm-blooded animals have **adapted**, or changed to suit, the places where they live. For example, there are foxes that live in very hot places, very cold places, and places with four seasons. The bodies of these foxes have adapted to protect the animals from different kinds of weather.

*Fennec foxes live in hot deserts. These foxes have very large ears. Large ears allow more heat to leave the body. They help fennec foxes keep cool.*

Arctic foxes live in the freezing Arctic. They have very small ears. Small ears keep heat inside the bodies of these foxes.

Red foxes live in many places around the world. The places where they live are warm in summer and cold in winter. The ears of red foxes are medium-sized. They are suited to both kinds of weather.

# Sleeping away winter

Some warm-blooded animals **hibernate** until winter is over. To hibernate is to fall into a deep sleep. Not only do the animals sleep, their breathing and heartbeats slow down and their body temperatures drop. Animals hibernate to save energy. They get energy from food, but there is not enough food in winter. Before hibernating, animals eat a lot of food to put on fat.

*Fat runs the bodies of animals while they sleep.*

*Arctic ground squirrels hibernate during the cold winter. They wake up in the spring. They are the only mammals that can lower their body temperatures to below freezing!*

# Not hibernating

Some animals sleep during winter, but they are not true hibernators. Bears, raccoons, and some prairie dogs are not true hibernators. They wake up several times to stretch their bodies or to eat some food that they have stored.

*Bears sleep in winter, but they do not hibernate.*

*These prairie dogs have been sleeping for months. They woke up to check for enemies.*

# Cold-blooded sleepers

Many cold-blooded animals live in warm places. They do not have to worry about cold winter temperatures. Some frogs, turtles, and snakes do live in places with cold winters, however. These animals must hibernate to survive. Garter snakes move underground in groups to sleep. Hundreds of snakes huddle together to keep one another warm enough to stay alive.

# Muddy sleeps

Frogs hibernate at the bottom of ponds or streams. They dig into the mud until spring warms the water again. The mud is much warmer than the water, and it has air bubbles. The frogs do not need much air because their breathing becomes very slow.

*This frog has woken from its hibernation. It is swimming out of the pond to find some food.*

# What is migration?

Both warm-blooded and cold-blooded animals **migrate**. To migrate is to move from one place to another. Many animals migrate because winter is too cold for them. They fly to warmer places to spend the winter months.

## Flying south

Canada geese are warm-blooded. They spend summers in Canada and fly south in the fall to warmer places in the United States and Mexico. The geese then come back in the spring to raise their **goslings**, or baby geese.

*This Canada goose is back home again. She has many goslings to look after!*

## Monarch migration

Butterflies are cold-blooded animals. Many monarch butterflies leave their northern homes in autumn to fly thousands of miles to California and Mexico. It is warmer in these places. When the monarchs arrive, they cluster together on trees and go to sleep. In spring, the monarchs fly north again. Each year, new monarchs make the trip, but the butterflies always know where to fly.

# How to be cool

*This girl is sweating and drinking water to cool herself.*

Warm-blooded animals need to cool off when their bodies get too hot. Some cool off by moving into the shade or into cold water. People wear thin clothing to feel cool. Some birds and mammals shed their winter coats for thinner fur or feathers. Some cool off by **sweating**. Sweating is losing water from the body.

*Hippopotamuses, or hippos, stay cool in water all day and come out of the water to feed at night.*

# Panting is cool!

Dogs and cats can sweat only through their feet. Cats lick their feet when they feel hot, but dogs **pant**. Panting allows water to leave dogs' bodies to cool them off. Birds pant, too. They also spread their wings to cool their bodies. Elephants flap their big ears like fans.

*This dog is panting to stay cool.*

*Some birds spread their wings to bring air to their bodies.*

*Elephants cool their bodies through their ears.*

# Cold-blooded cool-down

Cold-blooded animals also need to cool down when their bodies get too hot. Cold-blooded animals do not sweat or pant. Some cool off by moving into the shade or into water. Instead of lying flat in the sun, reptiles cool down by holding their bodies **upright**, or up and down. They get less sun that way.

*These baby alligators are cooling off in the shade. Their bodies are partly in water. The alligators are not lying down. They are keeping their bodies upright.*

# Life in hot deserts

Deserts are dry places. Animals need water to stay alive, but sometimes they cannot find enough water to drink. Desert tortoises can find very little water during the summer, so they must **estivate** for several months. Estivation is a kind of hibernation. Desert tortoises dig deep **burrows**, or holes, in the sand and sleep during the hottest and driest months of summer.

*The desert tortoise spends almost all of its time in its burrow. It sleeps through most of the winter, too. That's a lot of sleeping!*

# What do you know?

*polar bear*

*sea lion*

*dolphin*

*sea turtle*

Do you remember everything you learned about warm-blooded and cold-blooded animals? Test your memory by doing this quiz. There are six ocean animals on this page. Which three are warm-blooded, and which three are cold-blooded?

**Answers:**

**Warm-blooded:** dolphin, polar bear, sea lion

**Cold-blooded:** fish, sea turtle, sea star

*fish*

*sea star*

1. What covers cats and keeps them warm?

2. How do dogs keep cool?

3. How do you chill on a hot summer day?

**Answers:**

1. Cats have fur.

2. Dogs pant to cool off.

3. When you are too warm, you can sweat or get wet by jumping into a cool swimming pool!

# Glossary

Note: Some boldfaced words are defined where they appear in the book.

**adapted** Having changed something to make it more suitable to new conditions

**bask** To lie in the sun to take in heat

**blubber** A thick layer of fat on a sea mammal

**body temperature** The amount of heat inside an animal or a person's body

**burrow** A hole or tunnel dug by an animal

**constant** The same over a long period of time

**den** A wild animal's home

**huddle** To crowd together to stay warm

**living thing** Something or someone that is alive and needs air, sunlight, water, and food

**mammal** A person or warm-blooded animal that has hair or fur, a backbone, and is born live; female mammals make milk in their bodies to feed their babies

**migrate** To move from one place to another during certain seasons

**pant** To take short breaths to keep cool

**reptile** An animal with a backbone and scaly skin, such as a lizard, turtle, snake, or alligator

**shivering** Shaking to warm up when cold

**sluggish** Slow-moving because of low energy

**surroundings** Things and conditions around someone or something

**sweating** Losing water from the body

# Index

Printed in the U.S.A. - CG